Stephen Smith
June 2000

E. DiPopolo(?)
6/2000

THE SILVER LAKE LOVE POEMS

Emanuel di Pasquale

BORDIGHERA

Library of Congress Cataloging-in-Publication Data

di Pasquale, Emanuel
    The silver lake poems : poems / Emanuel di Pasquale.
      p.   cm. -- (VIA folios ; 21)
    ISBN 1-884419-32-1
    1. Italian Americans—Poetry. 2. Italian Americans. I. Title.
    II. Series.

PS3554.I625 S59   2000
811'.54—dc21   99-50002

© 2000 by Emanuel di Pasquale.

All rights reserved. Parts of this book may be reprinted only by written permission from the author, and may not be reproduced for publication in book, magazine, or electronic media of any kind, except in quotations for purposes of literary reviews by critics.

Printed in the United States.

Published by
BORDIGHERA PRESS
Purdue University
1359 Stanley Coulter Hall
West Lafayette, IN 47907-1359

VIA FOLIOS 21
ISBN 1-884419-32-1

OTHER BOOKS BY EMANUEL DI PASQUALE

POETRY

Genesis

TRANSLATIONS

Song of the Tulip Tree
by Joe Salerno
Sharing a Trip. Selected Poems
by Silvio Ramat
The Voyage Ends Here
By Carlo Della Corte

Two of these poems appeared in
The Journal of New Jersey Poets

Deepest thanks to W.E.T.

For Mary

The Silver Lake Love Poems

Emanuel di Pasquale

I.

Brother of Achilles,
you, sad face in your window,
lights behind you
"at dusk ... lonely man. . . ."

I can see you in your white shirt.

Try to see goodness in your friends.
(Even Agamemnon in his
thickheaded stupidity
had a feel for the gods.)

II.

I'll mail you a small
emerald ring — it is
from my mother's part
of the family — sea captains —
it is dark green — wear it
on your pinky,
but promise to dislodge
it while you fondle others.

Barter with me: send me a poem!

III.

Jesus, I'm alive!

My house is all blue
within and without
purple in Iris
and white in Carnations
red in Poppies
and my Blood.

(That morning the ocean
was the color of Olives —
your skin.)

IV.

I struggle in the mountains
thinking of you,
at times putting myself
in your small room next to the bathroom,
typing your poems,
playing my flute,
cooking eggplant,
arranging beach plums,
walking my small dog along the shore
at dusk.

V.

Treasure the divine in you,
the silences,
the look at the stars,
the lonely ocean swims at dawn,
your morning music,
Pavarotti singing Christmas songs in May,
your bare feet
on linoleum.

VI.

Crystal cut today, sharp, blue,
windy, long-shadowed. The lake glitters.

Awful at your reading. The sadness
of sitting behind your children.
And you wanting everyone, everyone
but me.

Oddly coarse looking your son's hair.
Yours. But soft to the touch.

Smooth and soft my daughter. Golden.
I wonder if I'm related to any
of the people in my house.

VII.

Revise your poems, Eman.
I like you when you're working,
polishing things, honing clean.
(But do apply for fellowships —
bend a little — make your life easier.
Even the Sainted Stafford works for money.)
Tomorrow I must cook turkey, squash, turnips, sweet potatoes —
pack, polish my riding boots, do my aerobics,
arrange for rabbits, turkeys,
deer, and cat to be fed
when I'm gone — do a million
laundries, iron — and write again to you
and think more about our story
(mostly in my head).

Oh, I finally planted
that other bag of Iris.
Cold winter is closing up; it will be a Spring,
"a new ... life."

VIII.

My daughter is "killing" me noisily —
money, new car I paid for,
that pink dress, and that. . . .

I own nothing or old things —
a house full of old family stuff;
even the 2 boats are second hand.

IX.

You always sound angry over the phone.
I'm flat-footed, Eman.
I don't tiptoe around feelings.
I want to deal with seeing you.
(I'm not some ice-block
female who weeps about loving you
yet doesn't see you nor write to you.)
It's your bed I want right now.

X.

I sent you yellow mums
for the Dead Souls Day. My
yellow mums are beautiful —
wanted a florist to share
my yellow light with you.

XI.

You with the winged feet,
don't be put off by me.
I am too old to change now
(except maybe in bed — will
get better with our "genital" love).

XII.

You remind me sometimes of a boy —
Like my son, you fall asleep
and wake up in mid-sentences.
You smell sweet and clean,
and you sleep quietly.
When you were last falling asleep,
your sleep jerks woke you up
(you squeezed my hand
and jerked you leg),
you sprang awake and asked me if I was all right.
I was more than all right.
(Is that why you packed your bags?)

XIII.

I played with my children
last night, wheeling under the stars.
The last one to get dizzy and fall
down won. Guess?

(You may keep or chuck this photo —
taken "before the fall"
sitting on a fence on a
Virginia horse farm. Even then
my ass was flat.)

XIV.

Walking along the north star
in the dark. Geese gossip.
Ice amoebas across causeway.
Deer in vacant lot.
The moon, only half a person,
has fallen down on his back.

XV.

Hey, you in your red socks
and red underwear — experienced yet naïve —
roll out of that Magic Barrel.
You, with that look of sympathy,
of vulnerability, in the eyes.
Of experience.

XVI.

Did you find a black glove
in your apartment anywhere?
Yesterday the secretaries found
my contact lenses in the bathroom.
I need mitten strings, leashes, padlocks,
anchors and lead lines on all I own!

I smell your scent everywhere —
I see your golden skin,
brown eyes, soft hair.

XVII.

Received your letter — lopsided on the paper,
like the pillows on your bed —
let's keep this slightly askew, my dear.

I am a slippery anchor,
one that won't catch hold
on the loose material
at the bottom of the lake.

Perhaps you are right — freedom is emotional movement —
but people fear being free —
oh, if you'd only let me anchor in you —

May our anchors both catch into the same ground,
and we swing on our moorings in the same direction —
freely, though, freely,
with a wide swing,
clear of obstructions and collisions.

XVIII.

As for your Doctor H., I have started
to read his chapter on "Human Armoring."
Beneficial therapy, indeed, but
in no way would I lie down disrobed!
Damn doctors and scientists
that insist
on reducing our hearts and souls
to: "do this and this" and you will be new.

We are more than charts and graphs
and a father's no or a mother's yes.

Let writing and love be therapy enough!
(Add music maybe and dance or graphic arts.)

I think happily of your pressing
me against the bathroom wall —
later of your love arc in my mouth
and after that of you moving slowly, deeply in me.

XIX.

The leaves are down now, and the lake sparkles
through the trees like a piece of feldspar. And you —
Hector, Hermes, Achilles — have you seen my silver
earrings? I have looked for them everywhere. I
remember seeing them on your bathroom floor, but
I thought I picked them up and put them in my
purse. They are my favorite earrings.
If you have them, please save them for me —
just in case we can break down another wall.

XX.

When I saw *The Iliad* on your bathroom floor, I
fell in love with you forever. Then I thought
about Achilles dragging Hector's body around
Patroklos' funeral pyre — why is that? Loss? Grief?
Pain? The gods that intervene to help out both sides —
to light Patroklos' pyre, to protect Hector's body
from dogs and decay? These things have
significance, Eman, don't they?

Your father shouldn't have died so young — and you only
an infant! I know you miss him, that manliness and
that masculine love in you life. But there is
you now.

XXI.

You in your living room — all that whiteness
and sun — taking your glasses off so
deliberately and putting them on the window ledge,
like Marlon Brando in *Last Tango* taking the gum out
of his mouth and sticking it under the ledge before his
very deliberate actions.

So, you with the wine-colored underwear,
be strong and brave, swift and steady.

XXII.

Listen, you — I remember you saying
you felt like puking after you made love
four months ago — and with me you were
sick to your stomach and headachy —
and you recoiled from me a number of times
and seemed eager to rush me away.
Too much too rushed: all that driving around,
all those copies of poems,
letters, the hope you gave me,
the coral. You are so full
of goodness, so boylike and generous.
Inevitable, inevitable that you
would make yourself sick.
I understand — myself confused
and mildly horrified at myself.

XXIII.

We began the morning with a sapphire sky,
and now it is tinfoil colored.
I'll probably be driving to VA in the rain.
I wish you would call.

Speak not so provocatively to me on the phone —
I can't function afterwards! What if someone
at home or at work will hear you say that your
"penis is unraveling?"

I wasn't kidding when I said I've been dead
for many years — I couldn't laugh or love,
or worse, cry when I needed to, or stop crying
when I wanted to — I have been in hell
for a long time. But when you — all breathless
and excited — plunked down next to me in Albany
and offered me a copy of your book ("Cheap, only
$5.95," he said), I *knew* I was in trouble.

XXIV.

You must understand — I adore my children
and they have always come first, for me, I guess,
not for them. I might die without them.
I might also die without my woods and flowers
and small dog. (When you walk on the beach,
I am walking in the woods thinking of you
walking on the beach.) I am part of these low
hills, this ash, oak, and hickory. I
know I have been too long at the edge
of this still glacial lake (where my mother
grew up), and I want to change, but, dear,
I cannot tear myself from here for good.
(Please tell those gods to quit
pummeling me.)

XXV.

I write with your pen in your apartment.
Why do I feel so free and relaxed here?
The sea? You?
Everything is bleached white by the sun and sky and sea —
What a sunrise! Mares' tails in the sky and a
rainbow smudge in one of the clouds right out of this
window — a covenant. Maybe a blessing.

I worry about your headaches.
Your padding around in the predawn
making little noises with your mouth and feet.
Yes, you are reticent.

Last night I was in a tunnel
that was leaking yellow and red liquid down the
walls. Then you were angry.
Then I walked out of the apartment but forgot the key.
Despair. But you had left a new one by the door for me.

XXVI.

Yes, I guess it is important that our genitals get it together — my dear — but I would also like to walk on that beach and look at the moon from the same spot you do. If we care enough about one another, the physical will be fine. We have to be patient and understanding, though. You know that. We have been with others for years and we can't expect suns-and-moons-and-stars so soon. Also, I worry about your lovely slender petite blond women, demure and quiet, not the give-you-a-headache type. And here I am with my loud whinnying laugh and a fast-paced walk (my students tease me about my fast walk and the sound of my highheels — coming out of my office I'm like a horse at the starting gate of a race). Dear, I just don't know how to be any other way. Maybe you can calm me down; put some shoes on my feet and a bit in my mouth ... a nice saddle, too. Don't expect too much ... I'm part peasant, too, and part lunatic.

XXVII.

You circling the parking lot,
looking, looking, looking
for something, someone;
you sitting on the corner of the desk
in the English department office
(a red bow tie and a London
Hard-Rock Café sweat shirt on);
you naked and gold
in your apartment, shapely,
no edges anywhere;
you in your shiny black
shirt at the wheel of your Honda,
your wrists and hands
(such thick veins,
such clean nails)
on the gear shift;
you, later, driving away, lost,
in your upturned collar and
the swirl of lights and darkness. . . .

About the Author

EMANUEL DI PASQUALE has published poems in *American Poetry Review*, *Sewanee Review*, and many anthologies and textbooks. BOA Editions published a volume of his poems entitled *Genesis*.

He has also translated numerous poets from English into Italian and from Italian into English. His translations include: *Song of the Tulip Tree*, by Joe Salerno, winner of the 1998 Bordighera Poetry Prize, a bilingual edition; *Sharing a Trip. Selected Poems*, by Silvio Ramat, forthcoming in the series *CROSSINGS*, from Bordighera Press; and Carlo Della Corte's *The Voyage Ends Here*, to appear with Gradiva Publications.